# What We Do in Church

## An Anglican Child's Activity Book

**Anne E. Kitch**

**Illustrations by Dorothy Thompson Perez**

Morehouse Publishing
NEW YORK · HARRISBURG · DENVER

Copyright © 2004 by Anne E. Kitch

Morehouse Publishing
4775 Linglestown Road
Harrisburg, PA 17112

*Morehouse Publishing is an imprint of Church Publishing Incorporated*

Stained glass images on page 10, "Song of Praise," from the Cathedral Church of the Nativity, Bethlehem, Pennsylvania. Rendered by Delores Schiesser.

Interior design by Beth Oberholtzer

Printed in the United States of America

08  09  6  5  4

# Worshipping with Children

Young children have a religious life. They come to worship already known and loved by God, and already knowing and loving God in return. The worship of children is pleasing to God.

As adults, it's important for us to acknowledge children as spiritual people with whom we might enjoy a conversation, rather than as empty vessels to fill with knowledge. This book is meant to be a tool—for parents as well as other Christian Educators—for exploring and talking with 2- to 6-year-olds about what we do in church. As with adults, the more children understand what is happening in worship, the more engaged they will be in worshipping. The activities on the pages of *What We Do in Church* are meant to engage both you and your child as you explore together the richness and power of Anglican worship.

ANNE E. KITCH
Canon for Christian Formation
*Cathedral Church of the Nativity*
*Bethlehem, Pennsylvania*

# How to Use this Book

This book is loosely divided into four sections: Sunday Worship, The Church Year, People and Worship, and Worshiping with Our Senses. The intent of all the activities is to help children be more aware of how we worship and how they can participate.

The activities in this book are best used one page at a time, rather than handing a child the entire book to color at once. The more interaction between a child and an adult when using the material, the more engaging the experience will be.

## Families

Parents and other family members can use *What We Do in Church* at home as adults and children learn together about worship. You may want to complete an activity page with your children on a Saturday evening in preparation for worship, as you talk about what you'll experience in church together the next day. After worship is another good time to choose an activity page that focuses on some aspect of your family's experience that day. You may also choose to bring an activity page to church for your children to use in the pew—the activities here can help them focus on what is happening around them. The pages are meant to engage children in worship, not distract them from it.

## Christian educators

Church school teachers will also find this book useful in a parish setting as a resource for church school classes and children's liturgies. The Sunday Worship activities could be used one each week as a group activity during a children's chapel to help children learn about the liturgy. The church year activities could be used as "take home" pages, with teachers giving children the appropriate page at the beginning of each church season to complete and discuss with their families. Any of the activities could be added to children's packets which some parishes have available for children to use during worship.

## Using this book with non-readers

Toddlers and preschool children respond to the world around them with their senses. They are aware of the things they see, hear, touch, and smell even before they have names for them and words to describe them. They can happily engage with the pages on their own with some crayons or markers. Then they can connect at a deeper level when an adult sits down and reads the pages to them.

## Using this book with readers

Early elementary children will enjoy reading the pages on their own. However, don't miss the opportunity of learning from them by initiating conversation about worship and their church.

Each activity in this book is meant to be a learning tool, not a quiz. Help children discover the answers to questions. For example, if you use the Advent page 24 during the season of Advent, you can ask children to look at and observe the color of the hangings and vestments in church, helping them discover the Advent color on their own.

# Welcome to Church

Connect the dots to see one way we welcome people to church.

# Welcome to Church

Draw yourself, your family, and your friends into this picture.

# Welcome to Church

Color God's people as they go out into the world.

# Follow the Worship Path

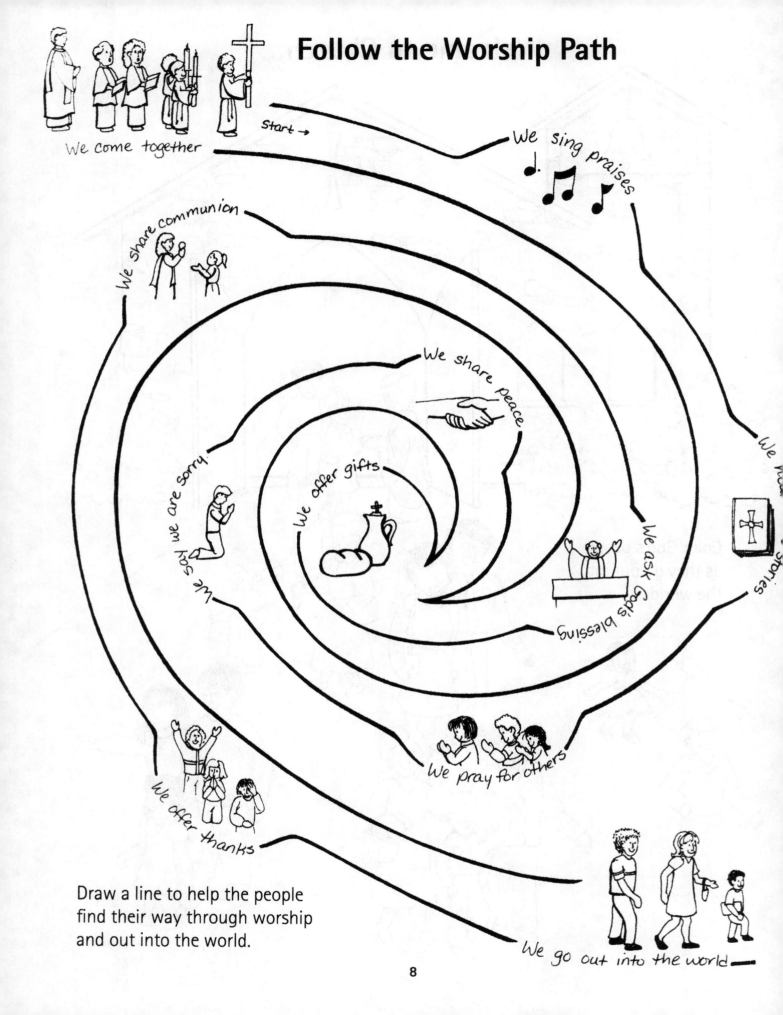

We come together

Start →

We sing praises

We share communion

We share peace

We say we are sorry

We offer gifts

We ask God's blessing

We read... stories

We offer thanks

We pray for others

Draw a line to help the people find their way through worship and out into the world.

We go out into the world

# The Procession

**acolytes**     **deacon**     **priest**     **crucifer**     **choir**     **bishop**

Matching: Draw a line from each word to the person it names in the procession.

# Song of Praise

Glory to God in the highest...

On the stained-glass windows, two angels join us in singing songs of praise. Color them. Are there stained-glass windows in your church?

# Readings

We listen to readings from the Bible, God's Holy _____. In church

we _____ to listen. We hear readings from both the _____

and _____ Testaments.

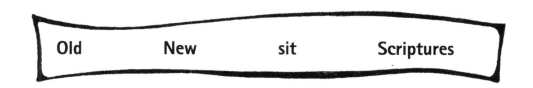

| Old | New | sit | Scriptures |

# The Gospel

We **stand** to listen to the Gospel, which means **Good News**. There are four different Gospels in the Bible called **Matthew**, **Mark**, **Luke**, and **John**. They tell us stories about **Jesus**.

Across:

2. The Gospel of L_ _ _ tells us about angels visiting baby Jesus.

4. One of the Gospels is called J_ _ _ _.

5. In church we _ _ _ _ _ _ to listen to the Gospel.

7. The Gospel of _ _ _ _ _ _ _ _ tells us about the Sermon on the Mount.

Down:

1. The Gospels tell us stories about _ _ _ _ _.

3. The word Gospel means _ _ _ _ _ _ _ _.

6. The shortest Gospel is called _ _ _ _.

# The Sermon

We _____ to listen to the sermon. The _____ tells us more about the _____ _____.

**Good News**          **preacher**          **sit**

Draw in the faces of the priest and the children as they listen to the sermon.

# The Creed:
# We Believe!

```
R U C H E V A
F H G O D I J
A E V L I F E
T A N Y G D S
H V E S O N U
E E B P A R S
R N L I B O P
C H U R C H T
J E R I F L Y
B A P T I S M
```

Find and circle these words

| | | |
|---|---|---|
| **God** | **Holy Spirit** | **Heaven** |
| **Father** | **Jesus** | **Church** |
| **Son** | **Life** | **Baptism** |

# The Prayers

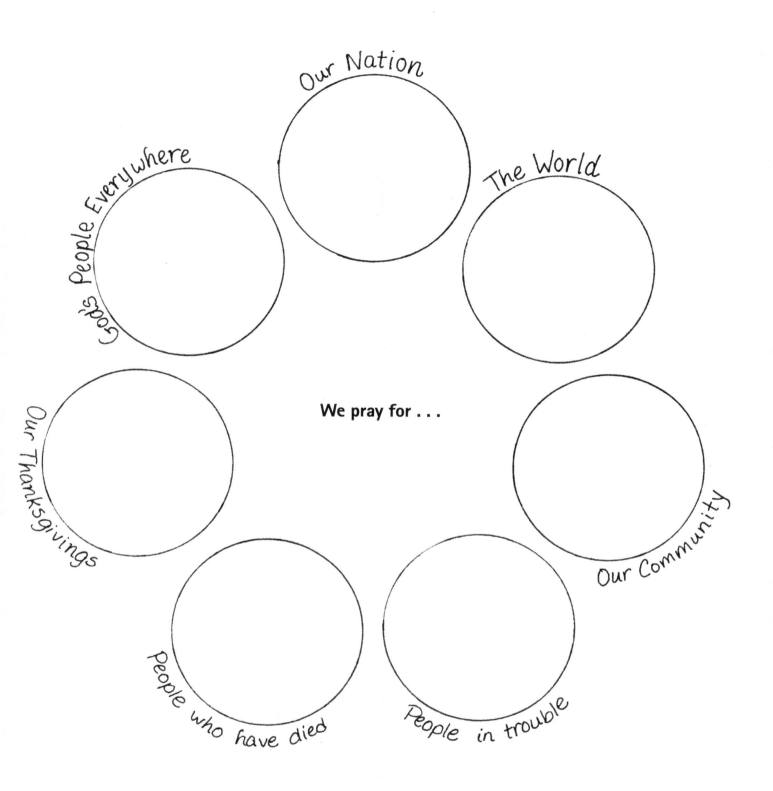

Our Nation

The World

God's People Everywhere

We pray for . . .

Our Thanksgivings

Our Community

People who have died

People in trouble

Draw your prayers in each circle.

# The Confession

During the confession we _____ our sins. We tell God we are sorry for any hurt we have caused. We ask God's _____. God promises always to _____ us.

**forgive**          **confess**          **forgiveness**

# The Peace

At the time of the peace we share God's peace with a hug or a handshake.

Draw more people sharing the peace.

# Offertory

We offer our gifts to God.

Draw some gifts that you would like to offer to God.

# The Great Thanksgiving

The priest calls us to pray together over the gifts of _____ and
_____ and offer our deepest _____ to God for everything.

thanks          bread          wine

Draw yourself and other people praying.

# The Breaking of the Bread

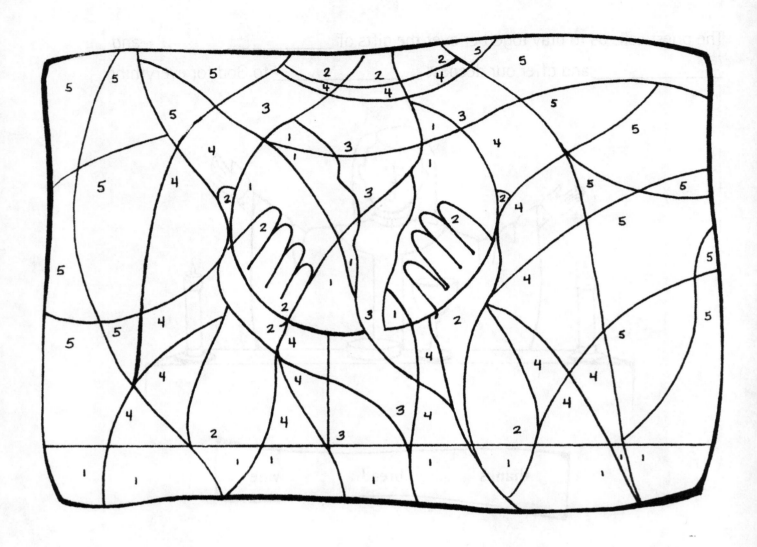

| 1 – yellow | 3 – blue | 5 – red |
|---|---|---|
| 2 – brown | 4 – green | |

Color by number to find the hidden picture.

# Communion

We receive the body and blood of Christ.

Draw the bread of heaven in each person's hands.

# The Blessing and Dismissal

Follow the path to do God's work in the world.

Start →

# Church Year Calendar

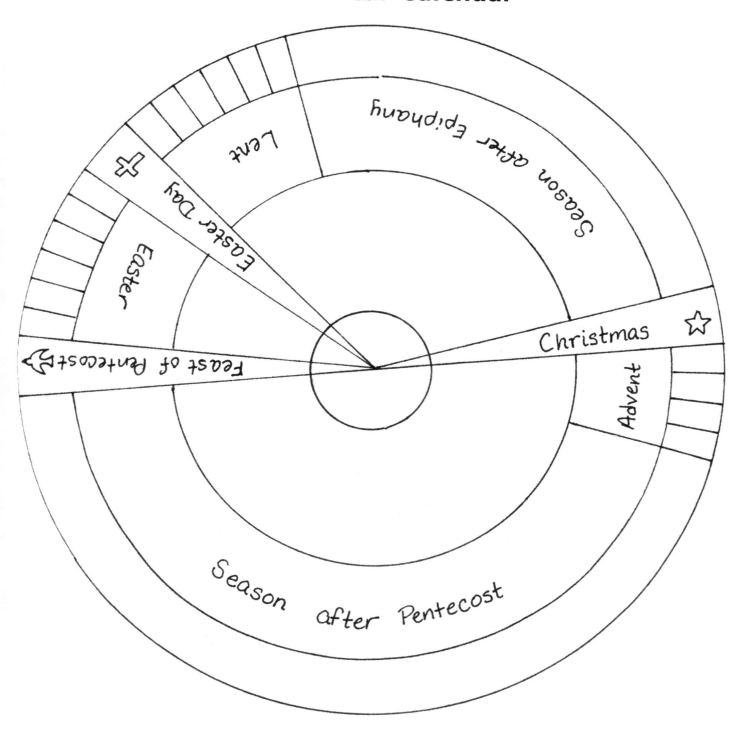

Each Church season has a different color. Color the seasons according to the key:

green – Season after Pentecost
and Epiphany

blue – Advent

gold – Christmas and Easter

red – Pentecost

purple – Lent

# Advent

During Advent, we use the color _____ in church. Advent is a time
of waiting for the birth of Jesus and for the return of Christ the King.

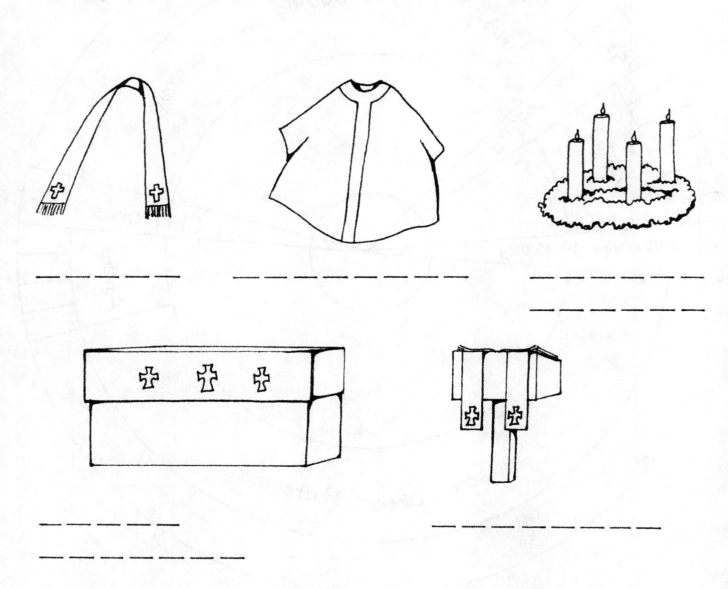

Write the names under the objects and color them the Advent color.

**advent wreath**          **stole**          **hangings**

**chasuble**          **altar frontal**

# Christmas

The Christmas season lasts for 12 days. Can you find 12 angels in the Nativity scene?

# The Epiphany

On January 6, we celebrate the feast of the Epiphany, when the Magi brought gifts to the child Jesus. (Matthew 2:1–12)

Follow the dots to find what the Magi followed to find Jesus.

# Ash Wednesday

Ash Wednesday is the beginning of _____. On this day we mark our foreheads with _____. This reminds us that God made the first person out of _____ and that all people die. It also reminds us that we belong to _____. On Ash Wednesday especially, we tell God we are sorry for our _____.

**sins      ashes      God      Lent      dust**

Draw a cross on their foreheads.

# Lent

Jesus was in the wilderness for 40 days and was tempted by Satan. We spend the 40 days of Lent preparing for Easter.

Help the girl find her way through the wilderness to the water of new life.

# Lent

Lent is a time of special prayer, giving to others, and living simply as we prepare for Easter.

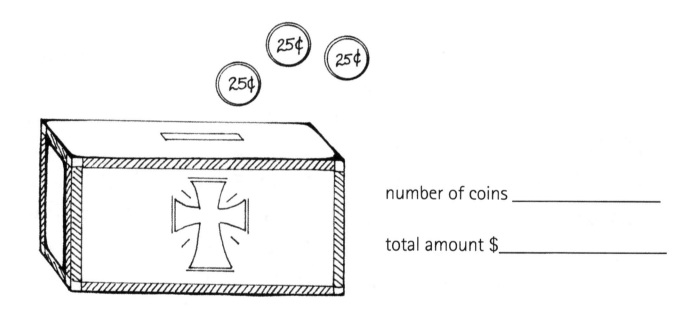

number of coins _____

total amount $_____

Count the number of coins going into the mite box. Draw coins that you would like to put in.

# Holy Week

Circle the numbered Holy Week words in the puzzle.

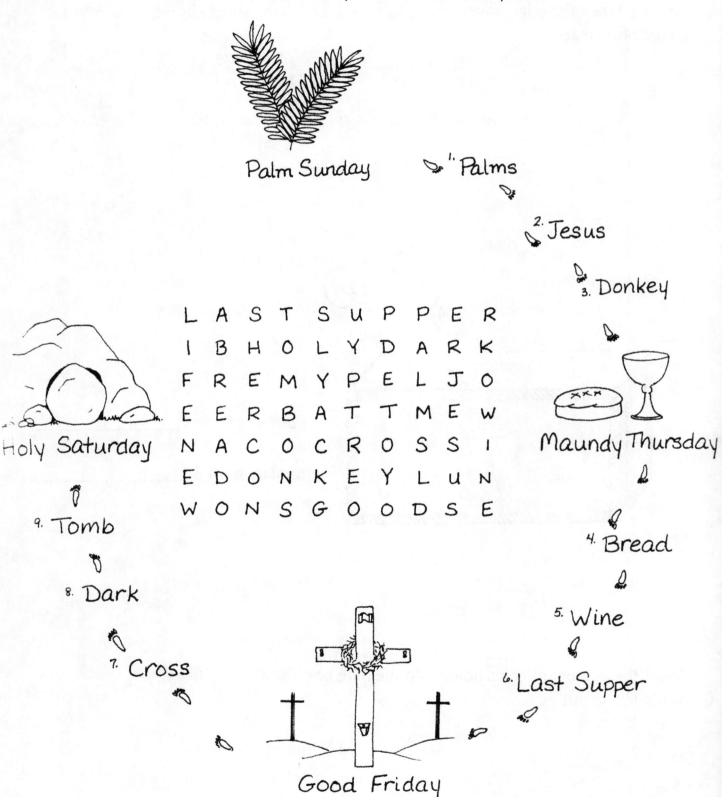

Palm Sunday

1. Palms

2. Jesus

3. Donkey

Maundy Thursday

4. Bread

5. Wine

6. Last Supper

Holy Saturday

9. Tomb

8. Dark

7. Cross

Good Friday

```
L A S T  S U P P E R
I B H O L Y D A R K
F R E M Y P E L J O
E E R B A T T M E W
N A C O C R O S S I
E D O N K E Y L U N
W O N S G O O D S E
```

# Easter Comes

In church we see signs of new life at Easter. Circle the things that have changed in the Easter picture.

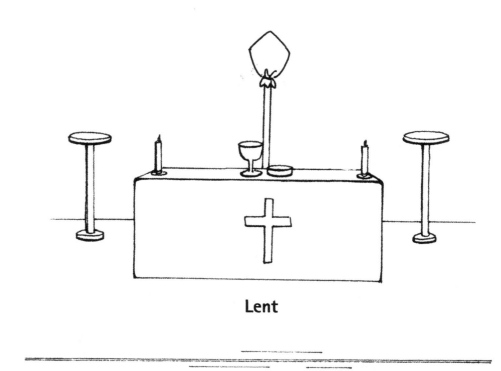

**Lent**

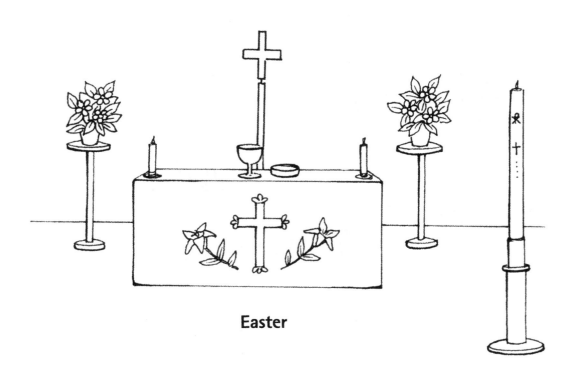

**Easter**

# 50 Day Party

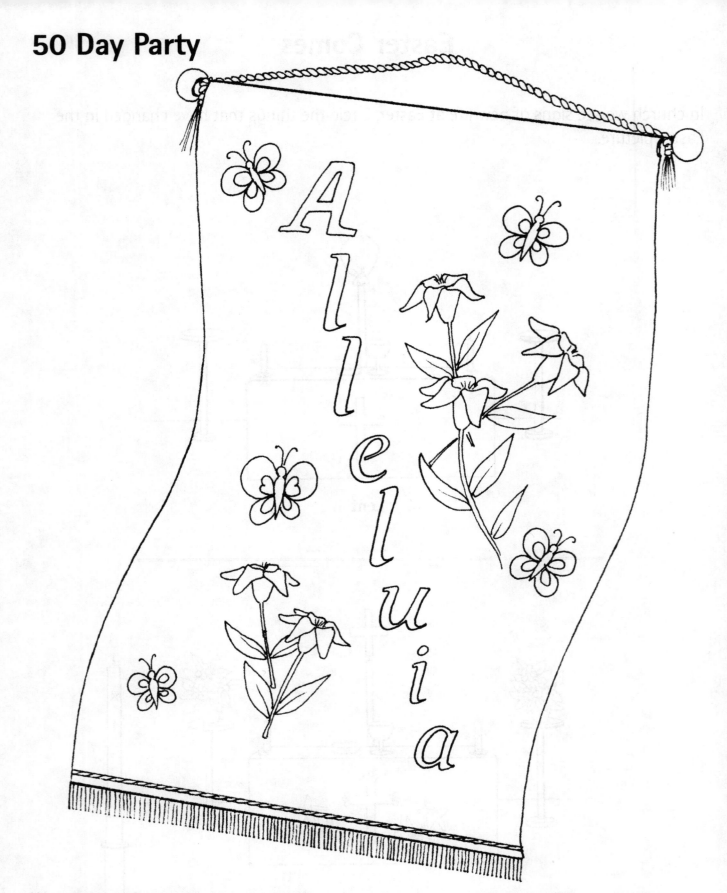

We celebrate Easter for 50 days by shouting Alleluia for joy. Color the Alleluia banner with joyful colors.

# Pentecost

On the feast of Pentecost, we celebrate receiving the gift of the _____
_____. The church color is _____ to remind us of _____,
one of the symbols of the Holy Spirit.

red          Holy Spirit          fire

Color the altar frontal and vestments in the Pentecost color.

# Many People Help With Worship

Match the name of the helper with the picture.

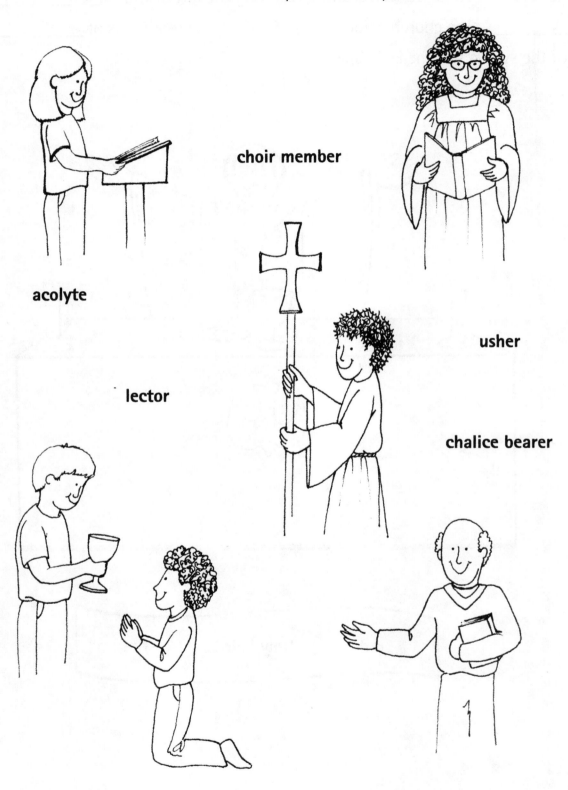

choir member

acolyte

usher

lector

chalice bearer

Circle the picture that show things you would like to do.

# Acolyte

**An acolyte wears**

**an alb**        **or**        **a cassock and cotta**

**a cotta is white**

**an alb is white**

**a cassock can be any color, often red or black.**

**a cincture is a rope belt**

What do the acolytes in your church wear?
Color the acolyte. Draw a picture of an acolyte
in your church.

# Deacon

A deacon wears

an alb

a stole over the
left shoulder

The alb is white; the
stole and dalmatic match the
liturgical color for
the season or occasion.

a dalmatic over
the alb

Color the deacons.

# Priest

A priest wears

an alb

a stole over both shoulders

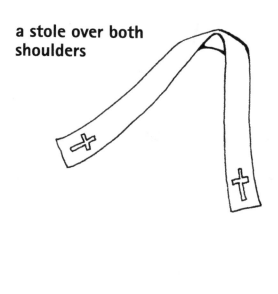

a chasuble over the alb

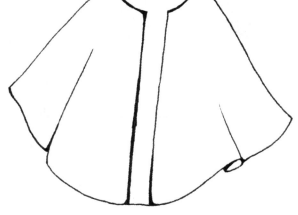

The alb is white; the stole and chasuble match the liturgical color for the season or occasion.

Color the priest.

# Bishop

A bishop wears

an alb

a cope – a large robe or cape

a stole

a mitre – a tall hat

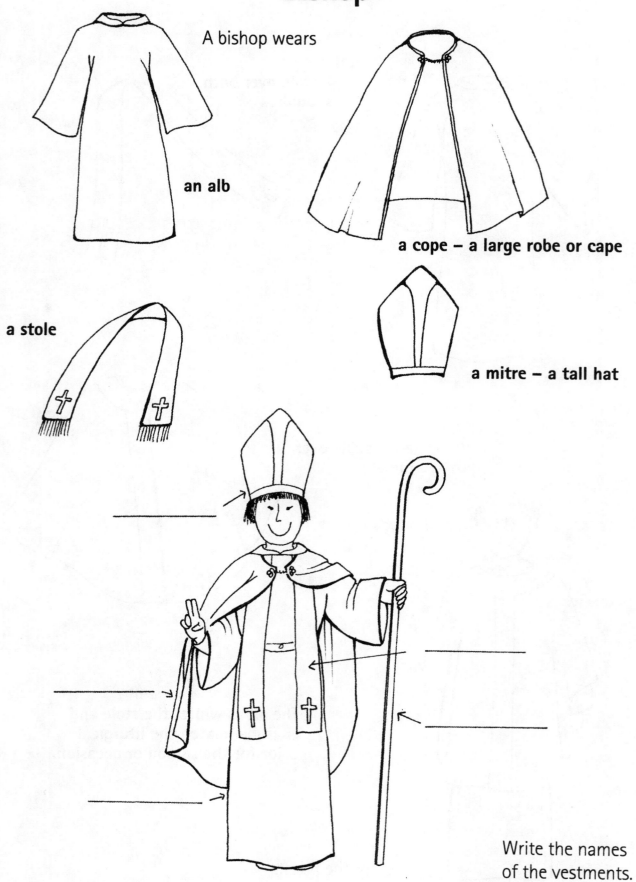

Write the names
of the vestments.

# Me

What do you wear to church? Draw a picture of yourself in your favorite church clothes.

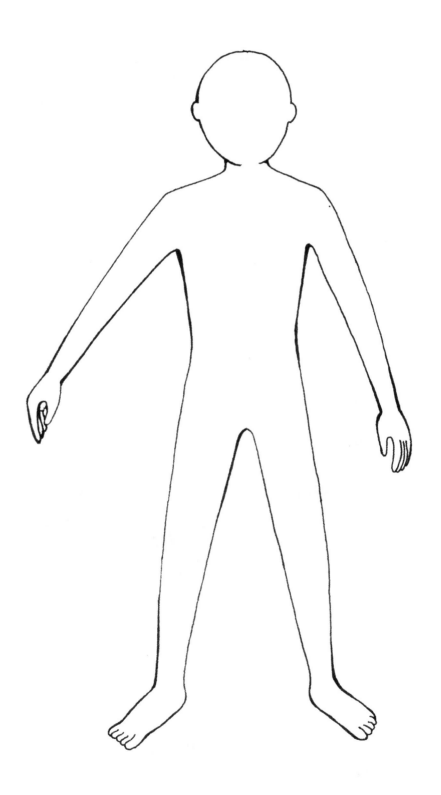

# We Worship with Our Senses

During worship what can you . . .

| See 👁 | Hear 👂 | Smell 👃 |
|---|---|---|
|  |  |  |

Place pictures in the column or columns where you think they belong.
Draw other things you observe with your senses during worship.

# We Worship with Our Bodies

We stand to sing or proclaim. We sit to listen.
We stand or kneel to pray.

**The Procession**

**The Lessons**

**The Gospel**

**The Sermon**

**The Creed**

**The Confession**

**The Prayers of the People**

**The Great Thanksgiving**

Draw a line from the part of the service to the picture of what you would do.

# Sacred Vessels

When we celebrate the Eucharist, it is a very special meal. We use our best dishes to honor Christ.

Decorate the chalice (cup) and paten (plate).

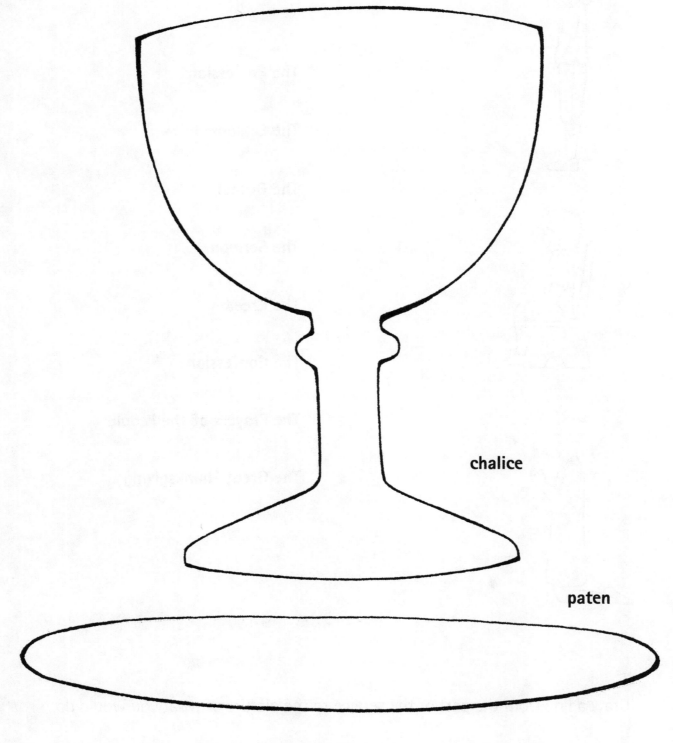

chalice

paten

# Set the Altar

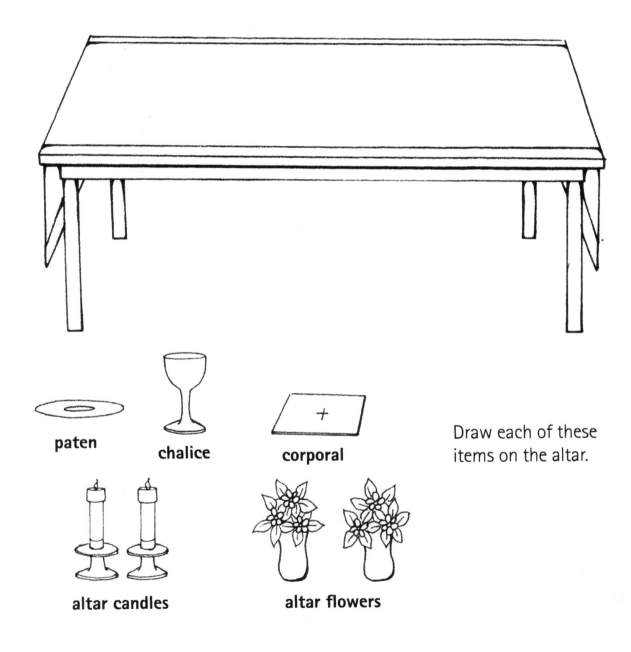

paten

chalice

corporal

altar candles

altar flowers

Draw each of these items on the altar.

# Trinity

Trinity means three. In church, the Trinity refers to our God, who is God the Father, Jesus Christ, and the Holy Spirit. We use symbols and pictures to represent God. Draw what you think God looks like.

Color these symbols and draw more symbols that you observe.

# Notes for Parents and Other Christian Educators

As we gather together for worship, we celebrate our belonging in the Body of Christ, the Church. *What We Do in Church* opens with three activities that remind children and adults alike that Church is not a building, but a community of believers. We welcome people into the Body of Christ through baptism, we nourish our life in Christ through communion, and we continue to live as members of the Body of Christ in our daily lives. As Christians, what we do in church reflects who we are as the Church.

## Part One: Sunday Worship

The first set of activities, on pages 8 through 22, take children through our celebration of the Eucharist, which follows a particular pattern. The Eucharist is divided into two main parts: The first is the Liturgy of the Word (the Word of God), in which we gather to hear God's story and the proclamation of the Good News of Jesus Christ. The second is the Liturgy of the Table (the Holy Communion), in which we pray for and receive the sacrament of Christ's body and blood. If you follow the service in the Book of Common Prayer, take note of the rubrics (those words that appear in italics), which explain what is happening during the liturgy.

Pages 9 through 17 follow the flow of the Liturgy of the Word. It begins with the entrance rite, which often includes a procession, then the Song of Praise (usually the *Gloria in excelsis* or the *Kyrie*), and the opening prayer, called the Collect of the Day. Next follow the readings from Scripture, including the Gospel reading. The proclamation of the Word continues with the sermon, the Creed, the Prayers of the People, the Confession of Sin, and the Peace.

Pages 18 through 22 focus on the Liturgy of the Table. This part of the service begins with the Offertory, in which we offer our gifts to God, including the bread and wine for communion and our contributions of money, as well as our anthems to praise God. The word "Eucharist" means "thanksgiving," so the prayer that is said over the bread and the wine is called "The Great Thanksgiving." It is through the prayers of the gathered community, presided over by the celebrant (a priest or a bishop), and the power of the Holy Spirit that the bread and the wine are blessed and become for us the sacrament of Christ's Body and Blood. The celebrant then breaks the consecrated bread. This action is called the "fraction," because the bread is broken, or "fractured." It is an important symbolic act that reminds us that Christ's body was broken for us, and that when we each take a piece of that broken bread, we are sharing in one bread and one body. The people then receive communion and offer a prayer of thanks. The final action of the Eucharist is the sending forth of the people. Worship does not end with us receiving the sacrament, but with us being sent out to be Christ's people in the world.

## Part Two: The Church Year

Activities on pages 23 through 33 take children through all the seasons of the Church Year. The Church Year really consists of two great feasts: Easter Day, a "movable" feast whose date changes from year to year, and Christmas Day, which is always celebrated on December 25. Easter Day is always the first Sunday after the full moon that falls on or after March 21. Based on these two feasts, the Church Year is divided into seasons: Advent, Christmas, Epiphany, Lent, Easter, and Pentecost.

Advent is the beginning of the Church year. "Advent" means "the coming"; the first Sunday of Advent is four Sundays before Christmas. During Advent we wait for the birth of Christ and we anticipate his second coming. The color for Advent is usually purple (for royalty) or blue (for peace). We celebrate Christmas, or the Feast of the Nativity, for 12 days, from December 25 to January 6. The color for Christmas is white or gold. January 6 is the Feast of the Epiphany, when we celebrate the visit of the Magi to the Christ child. The color for the Feast of Epiphany is white, but the Sundays following Epiphany are green. The Epiphany season runs from January 6 to Ash Wednesday and varies in length from six to nine weeks.

Ash Wednesday is the beginning of Lent. Lent is the forty days before Easter and is a time of fasting and preparation for the great celebration of Easter. The forty days represent the forty days Jesus spent fasting in the wilderness at the beginning of his ministry. The five Sundays in Lent are not considered fast days and are not counted in the forty. The color for Lent is usually purple (for royalty and penitence), but some churches use vestments in a natural linen with no color (for simplicity). Lent ends with Holy Week: Palm Sunday, Maundy Thursday, Good Friday, and Holy Saturday. The color for Holy Week is red.

The Easter Season begins with the Great Vigil of Easter on Easter Eve, followed by Easter Day, or the Sunday of the Resurrection. We celebrate Easter for fifty days, called The Great Fifty Days, until the Feast of Pentecost. On the fortieth day of Easter we celebrate Ascension Day, when the resurrected Christ ascended into Heaven. The color of Easter is white or gold.

The Feast of Pentecost is the last day of the Easter Season. We celebrate the coming of the Holy Spirit and the beginning of the Church. The color for the Feast of Pentecost is red (for fire and the Holy Spirit). The Sundays after Pentecost until Advent are called the Season after Pentecost. The color for this season is green (for growing and new life).

## Part Three: People and Worship

Activities on pages 34 through 39 introduce children to the people they see and hear during the celebration of the Eucharist. The celebration of the Sunday Eucharist invites the participation, in many different ways, of many different people. Among those people your children will see are members of the congregation, ushers and acolytes, lectors and chalice bearers, deacons and priests. All of us join together in praise and worship of God. With your child, look around and try to identify those who have a part in the service and talk about what they do to help make our worship experience meaningful and beautiful. What roles do children have? Take the opportunity to introduce your child to one or two of these participants before or after the service. Your child may want to ask them questions about their role.

## Part Four: We Worship with Our Senses

The activities on pages 40 through 44 will show children how we worship with our senses. In the Anglican tradition, we are intentional about what our bodies are doing, about when we stand or sit or kneel. We worship with our voices in prayer and song, with our ears through music and voices, with our eyes through symbol and visual beauty. We even engage our sense of smell through the perfume of flowers and incense. The beauty of our churches and our worship both honors God and draws us into a sense of God's glory. Most churches are full of symbols that engage us in worship and teach us about God. Sometime before worship, take a walk with a child through your church. What do you see, hear, smell? Are there stained glass windows? What stories do they tell? Are there Christian symbols on kneelers, furniture, or altar hangings? What do they represent? Are there memorials that tell stories about the parish and its people? All of these things testify to the glory of God and enhance the richness of our worship.

# Glossary

**Acolyte:** A person who assists with worship by helping at the altar. Sometimes called a server.

**Alb:** A simple white robe worn by lay and ordained people when leading or assisting with worship.

**Alleluia:** A word of praise that has been used by the Church since its earliest days. It comes from the Hebrew word *Hallelujah,* meaning "praise the Lord."

**Altar frontal:** A decorative cloth that hangs over the front of the altar; it is often decorated with Christian symbols. Its color usually matches the color of the Church season.

**Bishop:** An ordained minister who is the chief priest and pastor of a diocese.

**Cassock:** A fitted robe, usually black but sometimes red, purple, or blue, worn by lay and ordained ministers when leading or assisting with worship.

**Celebrant:** The priest or bishop who leads, or celebrates, the Eucharist.

**Chalice bearer:** A lay person who helps administer the chalice with the consecrated wine during communion.

**Chalice:** A large cup, often made of silver but sometimes of pottery or glass, used for the wine during communion.

**Chasuble:** A large oval garment without sleeves that a priest wears when celebrating the Eucharist. Its color often matches the color of the Church season.

**Choir:** A group of people who help with worship by leading the singing. The word also refers to the place in a church where the choir is placed.

**Cincture:** A cloth belt that is worn with a cassock. May also refer to a rope belt that is worn with an alb, although this is more formally known as a girdle.

**Cope:** A large beautifully decorated cloak worn by priests or bishops in processions and on formal occasions.

**Corporal:** A square white linen cloth placed on the altar cloth on which the chalice and paten are set for the prayer of consecration.

**Cotta:** A wide-sleeved, loose, white garment that is worn over a cassock. Used by people assisting with the liturgy, such as choir members or acolytes. It is shorter than the similar surplice.

**Creed:** A statement of the Church's beliefs. The Church uses two creeds in worship: the Nicene Creed and the Apostle's Creed.

**Crucifer:** An acolyte who carries the cross in procession.

**Dalmatic:** A rectangular vestment with loose sleeves, worn over an alb by a deacon in the liturgy. It is usually the color of the liturgical season or occasion.

**Deacon:** An ordained minister whose call is to serve the people and who assists bishops and priests during worship.

**Dismissal:** A sentence that sends the people forth, said by a deacon or the celebrant at the end of the worship. The people's response is, "Thanks be to God."

**Eucharist:** The service of Holy Communion, also known as the Lord's Supper, the Divine Liturgy, and the Mass. The word "eucharist" is Greek for "thanksgiving."

**Gloria:** The *Gloria in excelsis,* an ancient hymn of praise that is sung at the beginning of the Eucharist.

**Gospel:** A reading from one of the four first-hand accounts of the life and teaching of Jesus contained in the New Testament (the books of Matthew, Mark, Luke, and John). During the celebration of the Eucharist, the Gospel is read aloud by one of the clergy, preferably a deacon. The word "gospel" means "good news."

**Great Thanksgiving:** The central prayer of the Eucharist that is said by the celebrant and the people over the bread and wine to consecrate it. Also known as the Prayer of Consecration or the Eucharistic prayer.

**Hangings:** Decorated bands of cloth hung from the lectern or pulpit that match the liturgical color of the season.

**Lay person:** Any baptized member of the church. All lay people are considered ministers of the Church and are to represent Christ along with ordained ministers.

**Lector:** A person who reads one or both of the lessons before the Gospel.

**Mite box:** A small box that individuals use to collect coins for a specific ministry. Mite boxes are often used during Advent or Lent by the youth in a parish. The word "mite" means a coin of small denomination, like a penny. The tradition of collecting "mites" is based on the story of the Widow's Mite (Mark 12:41–44).

**Mitre:** A large hat worn by a bishop as a sign of office.

**Offertory:** The part of the liturgy in which the people offer their gifts to God. These gifts include the bread and the wine used for communion, money, the music of the choir, and our own thanksgivings. The offertory begins the liturgy of the table.

**Paschal Candle:** This large decorated candle is lit at the Easter Vigil and remains lighted for the Great Fifty Days. It symbolizes that Christ is the light of the world. After Easter Season, it is lit for Baptisms and Funerals to remind us of the Resurrected Christ.

**Paten:** A small plate, often made of silver but sometimes of pottery or glass, used for the bread that will be consecrated during the Eucharist.

**Priest:** An ordained minister who presides over the sacraments, especially Eucharist and Baptism, and is the chief pastor of a parish.

**Procession:** The movement of those people participating in the liturgy to the appropriate place in the church; for example, the opening procession at the start of the service or the Gospel procession before the reading of the Gospel.

**Stole:** A band of cloth, usually the color of the liturgical season or occasion, which is worn by a priest or bishop over both shoulders as a sign of office. A deacon wears a stole over the left shoulder.

**Surplice:** A wide-sleeved, loose, white garment that is worn over a cassock and falls below the knee. It is worn by clergy at services other than the Eucharist.

**Thurible:** A vessel that is used for burning incense that is carried in procession. The person who carries the thurible is called the thurifer.

# Further Reading

Charles Mortimer Guilbert. *Words of Our Worship*. New York: Church Publishing, 1988.

Gretchen Wolff Pritchard. *Alleluia! Amen: The Sunday Paper's Communion Book for Children*. New Haven, CT: The Sunday Paper, 1984.

Vicki K. Black. *Welcome to the Church Year: An Introduction to the Seasons of the Episcopal Church*. Harrisburg, PA: Morehouse Publishing, 2004.

www.ingramcontent.com/pod-product-compliance
Lightning Source LLC
Jackson TN
JSHW060310140125
77033JS00021B/640

* 9 7 8 0 8 1 9 2 2 1 0 5 6 *